## Other Mother Goose Rhymes

collected and illustrated by

Anne Rockwell

THOMAS Y. CROWELL, NEW YORK

AUTHOR'S NOTE

"Terence McDiddler, the three-stringed fiddler," "Little Nanny Button-Cap," and the "Three little ghostesses, sitting on postesses" are some of the lesser-known Mother Goose characters, but they are among the favorites shared by my family through the years. I bring their rhymes together here with the hope that every child can enjoy the verses both alone or with family and friends who share my family's love of the nonsensical.

Copyright © 1980 by Anne Rockwell
All rights reserved.
Printed in the United States of America.

*Library of Congress Cataloging in Publication Data*
Mother Goose.
Gray goose and gander
& other Mother Goose rhymes.
Includes index.
SUMMARY: A collection of over 50 well-known
and less familiar nursery rhymes.
1. Nursery rhymes.   2. Children's poetry.
[1. Nursery rhymes]   I. Rockwell, Anne F.
II. Title
PZ8.3.M85Rl   398'.8   79-6839
ISBN 0-690-04048-2   ISBN 0-690-04049-0 lib. bdg.
1   2   3   4   5   6   7   8   9   10
FIRST EDITION

For Oliver, Elizabeth, and Hannah

Gray goose and gander,
    Waft your wings together,
  And carry the good king's daughter
    Over the one-strand river.

Barber, barber, shave a pig.
How many hairs will make a wig?
Four and twenty, that's enough.
Give the barber a pinch of snuff.

Little Blue Ben, who lives in the glen,
Keeps a blue cat and one blue hen,
Which lays of blue eggs a score and ten;
Where shall I find the Little Blue Ben?

What's the news of the day,
Good neighbor, I pray?
They say the balloon
Is gone up to the moon.

Oh, that I were
>   Where I would be,
Then would I be
>   Where I am not;
But where I am
>   There I must be,
And where I would be
>   I cannot.

Fee, fi, fo, fum,

I smell the blood of an Englishman:

Be he alive or be he dead,

I'll grind his bones to make my bread.

Terence McDiddler,
> The three-stringed fiddler,

Can charm, if you please,
> The fish from the seas.

It's raining, it's pouring,
The old man is snoring;
He got into bed
And bumped his head
And wouldn't get up in the morning.

Bat, bat, come under my hat,
    And I'll give you a slice of
        bacon.
And when I bake, I'll give you
        a cake,
    If I am not mistaken.

I do not like thee, Doctor Fell;

The reason why I cannot tell.

But this I know, and know full well—

I do not like thee, Doctor Fell.

There was a little boy went into
a barn,
And lay down on some hay;
An owl came out and flew about,
And the little boy ran away.

Three little ghostesses

Sitting on postesses,

Eating buttered toastesses,

Greasing their fistesses

Up to their wristesses.

Oh, what beastesses,

To make such feastesses!

Oh, where, oh, where has my little dog gone?
Oh, where, oh, where can he be?
With his ears cut short and his tail cut long,
Oh, where, oh, where is he?

The man in the moon
Came down too soon,
And asked his way to Norwich;
He went by the south,
And burnt his mouth
With supping cold plum porridge.

Three wise men of Gotham

Went to sea in a bowl;

If the bowl had been stronger,

My story would have been longer.

The cock's on the woodpile
> Blowing his horn,
The bull's in the barn
> A-threshing the corn,
The maids in the meadow
> Are making the hay,
The ducks in the river
> Are swimming away.

If I'd as much money as I could spend,
I never would cry, "Old chairs to mend.
Old chairs to mend! Old chairs to mend!"
I never would cry, "Old chairs to mend."

The old woman must stand
      at the tub, tub, tub,
The dirty clothes
      To rub, rub, rub;
But when they are clean,
      And fit to be seen,
She'll dress like a lady,
      And dance on the green.

Little Poll Parrot
Sat in his garret
Eating toast and tea;
A little brown mouse
Jumped into the house,
And stole it all away.

Here am I,
        Little Jumping Joan;
When nobody's with me
        I'm all alone.

Simple Simon went a-fishing,
>For to catch a whale;
All the water he had got
>Was in his mother's pail.

Fishes swim in water clear,
Birds fly up into the air,
Serpents creep along the ground,
Boys and girls run round and round.

Little Jack Sprat
> Once had a pig;
It was not very little,
> Nor yet very big,
It was not very lean,
> It was not very fat—
"It's a good pig to grunt,"
> Said little Jack Sprat.

Tom, he was a piper's son,
He learned to play when he was young.
But the only tune that he could play
Was "Over the Hills and Far Away."
Over the hills and a great way off
The wind shall blow my top-knot off.

Robin Hood

Has gone to the wood;

He'll come back again

If we are good.

Who's that ringing at my doorbell?
      A little pussycat that isn't very well.
Rub its little nose with a little mutton fat,
      That's the best cure for a little pussycat.

Two little dogs
Sat by the fire
Over a fender of coal dust;
Said one little dog
To the other little dog,
"If you don't talk, why, I must."

The girl in the lane

That couldn't speak plain

     Cried, "Gobble, gobble, gobble."

The man on the hill

That couldn't stand still

     Went hobble, hobble, hobble.

Rub-a-dub-dub,

Three men in a tub,

And how do you think they got there?

The butcher, the baker,

The candlestick-maker,

They all jumped out of a rotten potato.

'Twas enough to make a man stare.

Hoddley, poddley, puddle and fogs,
Cats are to marry the poodle dogs;
Cats in blue jackets and dogs in red hats,
What will become of the mice and the rats?

Down with the lambs,
        Up with the lark,
Run to bed, children,
Before it gets dark.

Sally go round the sun,

Sally go round the moon;

Sally go round the chimney pots

On a Saturday afternoon.

Old Farmer Giles,

He went seven miles

With his faithful dog Old Rover;

And Old Farmer Giles,

When he came to the stiles,

Took a run and jumped clean over.

From here to there
To Washington Square;
When I get there
I'll pull your hair.

Hey diddle, diddle,
The cat and the fiddle,
The cow jumped over the moon;
The little dog laughed
To see such sport,
And the dish ran away with
the spoon.

Three gray geese in a green field grazing,
Gray were the geese and green was the grazing.

I went to Noke
But nobody spoke;
I went to Thame,
It was just the same;
Burford and Brill
Were silent and still,
But I went to Beckley
And they spoke directly.

How many miles to Babylon?

Three score and ten.

Can I get there by candlelight?

Yes, and back again.

If your heels are nimble and light,

You may get there by candlelight.

Doctor Foster went to Gloucester

In a shower of rain;

He stepped in a puddle,

Right up to his middle,

And never went there again.

Little Betty Blue
Lost her holiday shoe;
What can little Betty do?
Give her another
To match the other,
And then she may walk out in two.

St. Dunstan, as the story goes,
Once pulled the devil by his nose,
With red-hot tongs, which made
him roar,
That could be heard ten miles or
more.

Poor Old Robinson Crusoe!
Poor old Robinson Crusoe!
He made him a coat
Of an old nanny goat,
    What a clever fellow to do so!
With a ring-a-ting-tang,
And a ring-a-ting-tang,
    Poor old Robinson Crusoe!

As Tommy Snooks and Bessy

Brooks

Were walking out one Sunday,

Says Tommy Snooks to Bessy

Brooks,

"Tomorrow will be Monday."

Pussycat ate the dumplings,
Pussycat ate the dumplings,
Mama stood by
And cried, "Oh, fie!
Why did you eat the dumplings?"

Little Tommy Tittlemouse
Lived in a little house;
He caught fishes
In other men's ditches.

There was an old man,
And he had a calf,
And that's half;
He took him out of the stall,
And put him on the wall,
And that's all.

Barney Bodkin broke his nose,
Without feet we can't have toes,
Crazy folks are always mad,
Want of money makes us sad.

Taffy was born
> On a moonshiny night,

His head in a pipkin,
> His heels upright.

Pussycat Mole jumped over a coal
And in her best petticoat burnt a
great hole.
Poor Pussy's weeping, she'll have
no more milk
Until her best petticoat's mended
with silk.

Dickery, dickery, dare,
The pig flew up in the air;
The man in brown
Soon brought him down,
Dickery, dickery, dare.

Wee Willie Winkie runs through the town,
Upstairs and downstairs in his nightgown,
Rapping at the window, crying through the lock,
"Are the children all in bed,
> For now it's eight o'clock?"

If I had a donkey that wouldn't go,
Would I beat him? Oh, no, no.
I'd put him in the barn and give him some corn,
The best little donkey that ever was born.

There was an old woman
> Lived under a hill
And if she's not gone,
> She lives there still.

Swan swam over the sea,
            Swim, swan, swim!
Swan swam back again,
           Well swum, swan!

The moon shines bright,
The stars give light,
And little Nanny Button-Cap
Will come tomorrow night.

A man in the wilderness asked of me,
"How many strawberries grow in the sea?"
I answered him, as I thought good,
"As many red herrings as swim in the wood."

63

## Index of First Lines

A man in the wilderness asked of me, 62
As Tommy Snooks and Bessy, 49
Barber, barber, shave a pig, 8
Barney Bodkin broke his nose, 53
Bat, bat, come under my hat, 15
Dickery, dickery, dare, 56
Doctor Foster went to Gloucester, 45
Down with the lambs, 37
Fee, fi, fo, fum, 12
Fishes swim in water clear, 28
From here to there, 40
Gray goose and gander, 7
Here am I, 26
Hey diddle, diddle, 41
Hoddley, poddley, puddle and fogs, 36
How many miles to Babylon?, 44
I do not like thee, Doctor Fell, 16
I went to Noke, 43
If I had a donkey that wouldn't go, 58
If I'd as much money as I could spend, 23
It's raining, it's pouring, 14
Little Betty Blue, 46
Little Blue Ben, who lives in the, 9
Little Jack Sprat, 29
Little Poll Parrot, 25
Little Tommy Tittlemouse, 51
Oh, that I were, 11
Oh, where, oh, where has my little, 19
Old Farmer Giles, 39
Poor Old Robinson Crusoe!, 48
Pussycat ate the dumplings, 50
Pussycat Mole jumped over a coal, 55
Robin Hood, 31
Rub-a-dub-dub, 35
St. Dunstan, as the story goes, 47
Sally go round the sun, 38
Simple Simon went a-fishing, 27
Swan swam over the sea, 60
Taffy was born, 54
Terence McDiddler, 13
The cock's on the woodpile, 22
The girl in the lane, 34
The man in the moon, 20
The moon shines bright, 61
The old woman must stand, 24
There was a little boy went into, 17
There was an old man, 52
There was an old woman, 59
Three gray geese in a green field, 42
Three little ghostesses, 18
Three wise men of Gotham, 21
Tom, he was a piper's son, 30
Two little dogs, 33
Wee Willie Winkie runs through the town, 57
What's the news of the day, 10
Who's that ringing at my doorbell?, 32